ANTONIO

VIVALDI

CONCERTO

FOR

FOUR VIOLINS

AND

ORCHESTRA

B MINOR ◇ SI MINORE

OP. 3, NO. 10, RV580

To access audio visit:
www.halleonard.com/mylibrary

Enter Code
2144-8992-8148-5463

ISBN: 978-1-59615-202-1

MMO Music Minus One

EXCLUSIVELY DISTRIBUTED BY

HAL•LEONARD®

Visit Hal Leonard Online at
www.halleonard.com

Contact us:
Hal Leonard
7777 West Bluemound Road
Milwaukee, WI 53213
Email: info@halleonard.com

In Europe, contact:
Hal Leonard Europe Limited
42 Wigmore Street
Marylebone, London, W1U 2RN
Email: info@halleonardeurope.com

In Australia, contact:
Hal Leonard Australia Pty. Ltd.
4 Lentara Court
Cheltenham, Victoria, 3192 Australia
Email: info@halleonard.com.au

VIVALDI'S *Concerto for Four Violins*

Antonio Vivaldi (1687-1741) has come to be known as the grand master of the Italian Baroque Concerto form. And it was in 1711 that he made a breakthrough in the development of this nascent form, with the release of an opus of 12 concerti, entitled *L'Estro Armonico* (loosely translated as "Harmonic Inspiration"). In this set he transformed the form of the concerto into something cohesive, brilliant and tremendously satisfying to the listener. Though concerti by Corelli, Torelli and Albinoni had developed the form somewhat, and Vivaldi was heavily influenced by their work, this seminal group of concerti cemented the alternation of *Tutti-Solo-Tutti* structure as well as the broader fast-slow-fast movement sequence. It was a turning point in musical history and one which laid the groundwork for the modern concerto form.

Written for four violins, violoncello and string orchestra, the B-minor concerto, no. 10, is cast in three movements. The opening *Allegro* is filled with a sense of movement, and the interplay between the solo violins is masterfully crafted by the Italian composer. The second movement, the *Largo*, is far from austere or maudlin. It is still pulsing with life, and it is this trait that infuses the entire concerto. The third movement, another *Allegro*, rounds out the concerto with an assuredness and a masterful understanding of the importance of the solo instrument in relation to its partners, both in solo and ensemble contexts. The overall feeling is one of exhilaration and serenity somehow combined in a way unique to this Venetian 'Red Priest.' Bach would later make a famous transcription of this concerto in his Concerto for Four Harpsichords and Orchestra, BWV1065.

This MMO learning and performance edition gives every violinist the flexibility to play any solo part in this unusual work. Listen to virtuoso violinist Bojidara Kouzmanova perform the entire concerto—through the miracles of multitrack technology—in all its parts, then you choose which of the four solo parts to play and stand center stage with the Tempi Concertati Chamber Orchestra under Maestro Todorov for your own masterful performance. Better yet, invite three other violinists over and perform to the provided orchestra-only version of this classic. It's sure to be a performance to remember, and tremendous fun for all involved!

CONTENTS

CONCERTO GROSSO
for 4 Violins and String Orchestra
B MINOR ॐ SI MINORE
Op. 3 No. 10, RV580

Antonio Vivaldi
(1678-1741)

II

III

L'ESTRO ARMONICO

※❦※

VIOLINO II

※❦※

OP. 3, NO. 10
RV580

MMO 3177

CONCERTO GROSSO
for 4 Violins and String Orchestra
B MINOR 𝄞 SI MINORE
Op. 3 No. 10, RV580

Antonio Vivaldi
(1678-1741)

II

III

L'ESTRO ARMONICO

❧❧❧

VIOLINO III

❧❧❧

OP. 3, NO. 10
RV580

MMO 3177

CONCERTO GROSSO
for 4 Violins and String Orchestra
B MINOR ⚭ SI MINORE
Op. 3 No. 10, RV580

Antonio Vivaldi
(1678-1741)

II

III

L'ESTRO ARMONICO

VIOLINO IV

OP. 3, NO. 10
RV580

MMO 3177

CONCERTO GROSSO
for 4 Violins and String Orchestra
B MINOR 𝄞 SI MINORE
Op. 3 No. 10, RV580

Antonio Vivaldi
(1678-1741)

II

III

Engraving: Wieslaw Novak

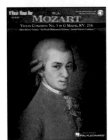
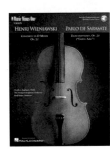
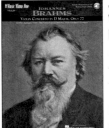

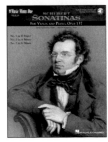